Dedication

To the testers who ask the hard questions, the develope
team that's ever rolled back a release at 2 a.m., and ever
a phase, it's a culture. This is for you

TABLE OF CONTENTS

Acknowledgments

Preface

Introduction

Chapter 1: Introduction to Test Automation

1.1 Evolution of Software Testing

1.1.1 Early Stages (1950s–1980s): Manual Testing and Debugging

1.1.2 Structured Testing (1980s–1990s): Formal QA Is Born

1.1.3 Automation Emergence (1990s–Early 2000s): The Tools Take Over

1.1.4 Agile and DevOps Era (2000s–2010s): Testing Becomes a Team Sport

1.1.5 The Modern Era (2010s–Present): Smart, Scalable, and Cloud-First

1.2 Benefits and Challenges of Test Automation

1.2.1 Key Benefits

1.2.2 Major Challenges

1.3 Key Industry Trends in Test Automation

1.3.1 AI and Machine Learning in Testing

1.3.2 Shift-Left and Shift-Right

1.3.3 Codeless Automation

1.3.4 API and Microservices Testing

1.3.5 Performance Engineering

1.3.6 Cloud-Based and Cross-Platform Testing

1.3.7 Visual and UI Testing

1.3.8 Mobile and IoT Testing

1.3.9 Blockchain and AI Testing

1.3.10 The Open-Source Revolution

1.4 Chapter Summary

Chapter 2: Building a Scalable Test Automation Strategy

2.0 Introduction: Why Strategy Matters

2.1 Defining Test Automation Objectives

2.2 Selecting the Right Tools and Frameworks

2.3 Applying the Test Automation Pyramid

Chapter 3: Scandium System Software – A Modern Approach to Intelligent Test Automation

3.1 Introduction to Scandium Automation Testing

3.2 Web Testing with Scandium

3.2.1 Overview

3.2.2 Key Features

3.2.3 Real-Life Use Case:

3.3 Mobile Testing with Scandium

    3.3.1 Overview

    3.3.2 Key Features

    3.3.3 Real-Life Use Case:

3.4 API Testing with Scandium

    3.4.1 Overview

    3.4.2 Key Features

    3.4.3 Real-Life Use Case:

3.5 Why Scandium Outperforms Manual Testing

3.6 Chapter Summary

Chapter 4: Choosing the Right Frameworks

    4.1 Framework Types: Data-Driven, Keyword-Driven, and Hybrid

    4.1.1 Data-Driven Frameworks

    4.1.2 Keyword-Driven Frameworks

    4.1.3 Hybrid Frameworks

    4.2 Behavior-Driven Development (BDD) with Cucumber

    4.2.1 Key BDD Concepts

    4.2.2 Benefits of BDD with Cucumber

    4.3 Page Object Model (POM) for UI Test Automation

    4.3.1 Key Concepts

    4.3.2 Benefits of POM

Chapter 5: Tooling for Test Automation

    5.1 Open-Source vs. Commercial Tools

    5.1.1 Open-Source Tools

    5.1.2 Commercial Tools

    5.2 Web Automation Tools: Selenium, Cypress, and Playwright

    5.2.1 Selenium

    5.2.2 Cypress

    5.2.3 Playwright

    5.3 Appium for Mobile Testing

    5.4 API Testing Tools: Postman and RestAssured

    5.4.1 Postman

    5.4.2 RestAssured

    5.5 Scandium System (Custom or Composite Framework)

Chapter 6: Industry-Specific Test Automation Approaches

    6.1 Automation in Healthcare

    6.2 Automation in Finance and Fintech

    6.3 Automation in E-commerce

6.4 Automation in Logistics and Supply Chain Systems

6.5 Automation in Telecommunications

6.6 Shared Patterns Across Industries

Chapter 7: Integrating Automation into CI/CD Pipelines

7.0 Introduction

7.1 Understanding CI/CD in Context

7.2 The Role of Test Automation in CI/CD

7.3 Key Features of Automation in CI/CD

7.4 CI/CD Automation Flow

7.5 Benefits of Integrating Automation into CI/CD

7.5 Tools Supporting CI/CD Testing

7.5.1 Jenkins

7.5.2 GitHub Actions

7.5.3 GitLab CI/CD

7.5.4 CircleCI

7.5.5 Azure DevOps

7.5.6 Bitbucket Pipelines

7.6 Common Challenges and Solutions

7.7 Version Control Strategies for Test Automation

Chapter 8: Performance Testing in Test Automation

8.0 Introduction

8.1 The Role of Performance Testing in Automation

8.2 Benefits of Automated Performance Testing

8.3 Common Types of Performance Tests

8.4 Tools for Performance Testing

8.4.1 Apache JMeter

8.4.2 Gatling

8.4.3 k6 (by Grafana Labs)

8.4.4 LoadRunner (Micro Focus)

8.5 Key Metrics to Track

8.6 Integrating Performance Testing into CI/CD Pipelines

8.7 Common Challenges and How to Overcome Them

8.8 Chapter Summary

9.0 Introduction

9.1 Self-Healing Test Automation

9.1.1 What is Self-Healing Automation?

9.1.2 How Does It Work?

9.1.3 Tools Supporting Self-Healing

9.1.4 Benefits of Self-Healing Tests

9.2 AI-Powered Test Generation and Maintenance

9.2.1 What Is It?

9.2.2 How It Works

9.2.3 Tools Offering This Capability

9.2.4 Benefits of AI-Generated Testing

9.3 Use Cases in Real-World Teams

9.4 Ethical Considerations in AI Testing

9.5 Limitations of AI in Test Automation

9.6 Chapter Summary

10.0 Introduction

10.1 Managing Flaky Tests

10.1.1 Identify and Isolate Flaky Tests

10.1.2 Common Causes of Flaky Tests

10.1.3 Fixing Flaky Tests

10.2 Refactoring and Optimizing Automation Scripts

10.2.1 Refactoring Strategies

10.2.2 Optimization Techniques

10.3 Real-World Example

10.4 Chapter Summary

11.0 Introduction

11.1 AI-Driven Testing, Low-Code Automation, and Robotic Process Automation (RPA)

11.1.1 AI-Driven Testing

11.1.2 Low-Code Test Automation

11.1.3 Robotic Process Automation (RPA)

11.2 Quantum Computing and Its Implications for Test Automation

11.2.1 What is Quantum Computing?

11.2.2 Implications for Test Automation

11.3 Preparing for the Future of Test Automation

11.4 Chapter Summary

REFERENCES

LEAVE A REVIEW

ABOUT THE AUTHOR

Acknowledgments

Creating this book was a journey of code, coffee, and collaboration. I owe deep gratitude to the engineers, testers, product owners, and thought leaders who inspired these pages, especially those who challenged conventional wisdom and asked better questions.

Special thanks to the mentors who taught me to prioritize clarity over cleverness. To my colleagues, reviewers, and early readers: thank you for your feedback, your debates, and your patience. To my family and friends, thank you for your unwavering support and understanding through long nights and tight deadlines. To the open-source community and the Scandium ecosystem: your innovation continues to raise the bar for us all.

And to Mr. Lawrence Samuel Temidayo, thank you for your guidance, encouragement, and belief in the vision behind this work.

And finally, to every reader, thank you for investing your time. I hope this book repays that investment many times over.

Preface

Let's be honest, test automation can feel like a minefield. One minute you're building fast, reliable tests, and the next you're knee-deep in flaky scripts, broken pipelines, and endless debugging.

This book emerged from that reality. It's not just a collection of tools or trends. It's a hands-on, experience-backed guide for anyone who's ever wrestled with the complexities of automation and thought. There must be a better way.

Whether you're a tester trying to scale your efforts, a developer tired of brittle code, a tech lead planning your team's next big move, or someone just getting started, this book is for you. It's meant to meet you where you are, and help you level up.

The strategies, frameworks, and examples here come from real-world challenges—the kind we face under tight deadlines, with limited resources, and high expectations. I've written this to be practical, clear, and above all, useful.

If this book helps make your work easier, your systems more stable, or your nights less stressful, then it's done its job.

Introduction

Why This Book?

Testing today isn't what it was 5 years ago. With microservices, continuous deployment, and user expectations higher than ever, the old ways of testing, slow, manual, and isolated, just don't cut it. Test automation has come a long way, from brittle scripts to AI-powered workflows, but the foundational question remains: Are we testing the right things, the right way, at the right time?

It's not just about which tool to pick or what framework to copy. It's about: Building systems that don't break under scale, integrating testing into every commit, build, and deploy, using AI and performance data to test smarter, not just harder. This book isn't about automating everything. It's about automating wisely.

I've seen too many teams fall into the trap of chasing coverage percentages while ignoring reliability or maintainability. That's why this book emphasizes strategy over volume, scalability over quick fixes, and quality over quantity.

What You'll Learn

Inside, we explore:

- The evolution of software testing and where automation fits in today's DevOps pipelines.
- Practical frameworks—from BDD to POM to hybrid systems.
- Deep dives into tooling for web, mobile, API, and performance testing.
- Cutting-edge trends like AI in testing, visual validation, and self-healing automation.

Each chapter is packed with hands-on examples, field insights, and principles to help you avoid common pitfalls and build automation that lasts.

Chapter 1: Introduction to Test Automation

"If you're not testing, you're guessing. If you're not automating, you're falling behind."

1.1 Evolution of Software Testing

Software testing didn't start as a discipline — it evolved out of necessity. In its early stages, it was a reactive process, primarily focused on debugging and defect discovery. Today, it's a proactive, integrated function embedded across the entire software development lifecycle (SDLC). Let's walk through that journey.

1.1.1 Early Stages (1950s–1980s): Manual Testing and Debugging

In the early days of mainframe computing, testing was mostly ad hoc and informal. Developers were responsible for their code, and testing usually meant "running it to see if it crashed."

- **No separation between coding and testing.**
- **No tools**, not even rudimentary logging, in many cases.
- Focus was on basic verification, not quality assurance.

💬 *Think about it: these were the days of punch cards and command-line assembly. Testing was survival, not strategy.*

1.1.2 Structured Testing (1980s–1990s): Formal QA Is Born

As software systems grew in complexity (and business impact), structured testing became a necessity. Testing got its seat at the table — and its teams.

- Introduction of **Waterfall methodology** and **systematic testing phases**.
- Test case documentation became standard practice.
- QA roles formalized within IT and product organizations.

This period laid the foundation for test design techniques we still use today: boundary value analysis, equivalence partitioning, and state transition testing.

1.1.3 Automation Emergence (1990s–Early 2000s): The Tools Take Over

Here comes the tools! With the rise of client-server and GUI applications, manual testing hit its limits. Automation was introduced to keep up with fast-growing test suites and shrinking delivery timelines.

- **Tools like WinRunner, QTP, and SilkTest** gained traction.
- Record-and-playback testing became common, but often brittle.
- Scripts broke frequently when UI components changed.

These tools were helpful but high maintenance. Automation was fast, until it wasn't.

1.1.4 Agile and DevOps Era (2000s–2010s): Testing Becomes a Team Sport

With the rise of Agile and DevOps, testing shifted left, becoming an integral part of development rather than an afterthought. Automation became essential for CI/CD pipelines.

- **Selenium WebDriver, JUnit, TestNG, and Appium** revolutionized open-source automation.

- Teams began using **CI tools** like Jenkins, GitLab CI, and Bamboo.

- Developers and testers collaborated more closely, often writing tests side-by-side.

Automation now supports iterative development. Testing was no longer "just QA's job."

1.1.5 The Modern Era (2010s–Present): Smart, Scalable, and Cloud-First

We're in an age where testing is intelligent, integrated, and infrastructure-agnostic.

- **AI/ML enhancements** (like self-healing tests and smart test selection) are becoming mainstream.

- **Codeless tools** are making automation more accessible (but not always more powerful).

- **Cloud-based test labs** offer massive scalability for cross-browser and cross-device testing.

- **Shift-right testing** allows teams to monitor performance and behavior *in production*.

The modern tester is part developer, part data scientist, part infrastructure engineer, and fully embedded in the team.

1.2 Benefits and Challenges of Test Automation

Test automation can save teams thousands of hours, catch critical regressions, and unlock scalable, fast-paced delivery. But it's not a silver bullet, it has actual costs and pitfalls if misused.

1.2.1 Key Benefits

Benefit	Description
Speed & Efficiency	Run hundreds of tests in minutes, perfect for regression and smoke testing.
Reusability	Frameworks allow teams to reuse and extend scripts across releases.
Accuracy	Reduces human error in repetitive validation tasks.
Scalability	Parallel execution on cloud devices and containers scales testing fast.
Cost-Effectiveness	Long-term ROI outweighs upfront investments when well-managed.

CI/CD Integration	Tests can be run on every commit, build, or merge request.
Enhanced Coverage	Enables coverage of edge cases, performance, and security, often missed manually.

1.2.2 Major Challenges

Challenge	Description
Initial Investment	Tools, infrastructure, and training can be costly upfront.
Maintenance Overhead	UI changes often break automated scripts (flaky tests).
False Positives/Negatives	Poor assertions or unstable environments cause misleading results.
Tool Selection Complexity	Choosing between Selenium, Cypress, Playwright, etc., can be daunting.
Skill Gap	Automation requires solid scripting and engineering know-how.
Non-Automatable Tests	UX testing, exploratory testing, and accessibility reviews still need humans.
Test Data Management	Creating realistic, safe, and reusable data sets is a major challenge.

Good automation isn't about automating everything — it's about automating the right things, in the right way.

1.3 Key Industry Trends in Test Automation

The test automation ecosystem is rapidly evolving. Here are the trends shaping the future of quality engineering:

1.3.1 AI and Machine Learning in Testing

- **Self-healing locators**: Automatically update when UI changes.
- **AI-based test generation**: Tools like Testim and Mabl generate tests from user behavior or code analysis.
- **Risk-based test prioritization**: ML models predict which tests are most likely to catch defects.

1.3.2 Shift-Left and Shift-Right

- **Shift-left**: Involve testers earlier — unit tests, static analysis, code coverage, contract testing.
- **Shift-right**: In-production testing, canary releases, A/B tests, and observability-based validations.

1.3.3 Codeless Automation

- Tools like **Katalon, TestSigma, and Tosca** help business users participate in automation.
- Faster to get started but sometimes limited in extensibility and debugging.

1.3.4 API and Microservices Testing

- Rise of **Postman**, **RestAssured**, and **Karate DSL** for service testing.

- **Contract testing** (e.g., using Pact) ensures microservices adhere to expected schemas.

1.3.5 Performance Engineering

- Tools: **JMeter**, **k6**, **Gatling**, and **LoadRunner**.

- Includes **real user monitoring (RUM)**, synthetic transactions, and SLA validation.

1.3.6 Cloud-Based and Cross-Platform Testing

- BrowserStack, Sauce Labs, and LambdaTest provide scalable browser/device matrices.

- Supports **parallel test execution** and **zero-infrastructure setups**.

1.3.7 Visual and UI Testing

- Tools like **Applitools Eyes**, **Percy**, and **Chromatic** detect visual regressions and layout issues.

- Crucial for **responsive designs** and **component-based UIs**.

1.3.8 Mobile and IoT Testing

- Tools: **Appium**, **Espresso**, **XCUITest**, **Detox**.

- IoT testing involves hardware-software interfaces, emulators, and simulation labs.

1.3.9 Blockchain and AI Testing

- Smart contract testing with **Truffle**, **Hardhat**, and **Ganache**.

- Testing AI models for fairness, reproducibility, and bias using toolkits like **Fairlearn** and **IBM AIF360**.

1.3.10 The Open-Source Revolution

- Tools like **Selenium**, **Cypress**, **Playwright**, and **Robot Framework** have thriving communities.

- Open-source tools offer transparency, extensibility, and faster innovation.

1.4 Chapter Summary

- Software testing has matured from informal debugging to AI-enhanced, cloud-scalable automation.

- Automation offers significant speed and scale benefits but requires thoughtful investment and planning.
- Understanding trends like shift-left, AI testing, and cloud platforms is essential to future-proof your skills.

🔧 Real-World Tip

"Don't automate for the sake of automation. Automate what matters, what slows you down, what breaks often, and what can be reliably repeated."

Chapter 2: Building a Scalable Test Automation Strategy

A roadmap to designing resilient, efficient, and future-proof automation systems.

2.0 Introduction: Why Strategy Matters

Test automation without a strategy is like coding without architecture; you might get things working but maintaining them long-term becomes a nightmare. Many teams rush to automate everything without defining *what*, *why*, or *how*. The result? Flaky tests, fragile pipelines, and disillusioned engineers.

This chapter helps you take a step back and build a **structured, scalable test automation strategy** that aligns with business goals, supports growth, and evolves with your software.

We'll explore:

- Defining automation objectives that move the needle

- Choosing tools and frameworks your team can live with (and grow into)

- Applying the test automation pyramid for maximum value with minimum chaos

Whether you're starting from scratch or recalibrating a bloated test suite, this chapter will guide you toward strategic automation success.

2.1 Defining Test Automation Objectives

Before you write a single test script, define *why* you're automating. Too many automation projects fail because the team never clarified their end goals. Automation isn't a checkbox, it's an investment. To see actual returns, objectives must align with both technical and business priorities.

🔍 Key Objectives of Test Automation

Objective	Why It Matters
Improve Test Coverage	Automate high-volume, repetitive scenarios that are time-consuming manually.
Increase Testing Speed	Accelerates regression and shortens release cycles.
Enhance Accuracy	Reduces human error in critical workflows.
Reduce Long-Term Costs	Once set up, automation saves time and lowers repetitive labor costs.
Support Continuous Testing	Enables CI/CD pipelines with constant validation of builds.

Real Talk: Don't automate just to say you did it. Automate because it solves a real bottleneck in your delivery flow.

Steps to Define Clear Objectives

1. **Assess Current Testing Gaps**
   - Are releases delayed due to long manual test cycles?
   - Are bugs being caught late (or worse, in production)?

2. **Align with Business Priorities**
   - Is the business prioritizing faster releases? Higher quality? Cost-cutting?

3. **Define Measurable KPIs**
   - Metrics like **defect escape rate**, **automation coverage**, and **execution time** give direction and track success.

4. **Prioritize What to Automate**
   - Focus on **high-risk**, **high-repeatability**, and **stable** areas first.

☑ *Pro Tip:* Start small. Win trust with quick automation wins before scaling up.

2.2 Selecting the Right Tools and Frameworks

Tool selection is one of the most politicized and debated steps in automation strategy. Every team has preferences; some want full-code control, others prefer codeless tools. The "best" tool is the one that fits your context: tech stack, team skill set, app type, and scalability goals.

Criteria for Smart Tool Selection

Choosing the right automation tool isn't just about what's trending; it's about what fits your team, your app, and your long-term goals. Here are some essential factors to consider as you evaluate your options:

Start by looking at **technology compatibility**. Does the tool support your application's tech stack? Whether you're testing a React-based web app, a native Android/iOS mobile app, or APIs for microservices, the tool needs to speak the same language — literally.

Next, think about **CI/CD integration**. Modern automation isn't a siloed activity; it needs to plug into your development pipeline. Can the tool integrate smoothly with platforms like Jenkins, GitHub Actions, Azure DevOps, or Bitbucket Pipelines? The tighter the integration, the easier it is to build a seamless testing workflow.

Consider the **learning curve**. A tool is only as effective as your team's ability to use it. Does it require deep programming expertise? Or can QA engineers and non-dev testers pick it up relatively quickly? Strike a balance between flexibility and accessibility.

Don't overlook **community and vendor support**. Is there strong documentation? Are bugs quickly addressed in public repositories? Is there an active forum or Slack community? A vibrant ecosystem around a tool can be a lifesaver when you hit unexpected issues.

Cost is always part of the equation. While open-source tools like Selenium, Cypress, or Playwright are free to use, they may require more setup and maintenance. On the other hand, commercial solutions like TestComplete or Tosca come with a price tag but often include enterprise support, dashboards, and built-in integrations.

Finally, assess **scalability**. Can the tool grow with your test suite? Can it run tests in parallel, across environments, and integrate with cloud-based test execution platforms? A tool that fits now but fails to scale later becomes a bottleneck.

Pro tip: Don't just choose tools based on popularity. Choose what solves your team's current pains while leaving room for future growth.

🖥 Popular Tools and Frameworks by Category

Category	Tools/ Frameworks	Best For
Web UI Testing	Selenium, Cypress, Playwright, Scandium	Browser automation, UI Validation
API Testing	Postman, RestAssured, Karate DSL, Scandium	Contract and functional API testing
Mobile Testing	Appium, Espresso, XCUITest, Scandium	Native/hybrid mobile app testing
Performance	JMeter, Gatling, LoadRunner	Load, stress, spike testing
BDD	Cucumber, SpecFlow, Behave	Business-readable tests via Gherkin

Framework Design Patterns

Type and Description

- **Modular:** Reusable test blocks; supports maintainability
- **Data-Driven:** Separates test logic and test data for flexibility
- **Keyword-Driven:** Uses readable keywords; useful for non-programmers
- **Hybrid:** Combines multiple approaches for scalability

Pro Insight: Whichever you choose, invest early in **good folder structure**, **naming conventions**, and **logging/reporting**. It saves headaches down the road.

2.3 Applying the Test Automation Pyramid

Introduced by Mike Cohn, the test automation pyramid is a foundational concept for efficient testing strategy. It guides teams on *where* to place their testing focus for the best ROI.

The Pyramid Breakdown

Layer	Coverage %	Tools & Purpose
Unit Tests (Base)	~70%	JUnit, pytest - Validate individual methods/functions.
Integration/API Tests	~20%	Postman, Karate - Test communication between services.
UI Tests (Top)	~10%	Selenium, Playwright - Validate user workflows visually but is usually slower and more fragile.

Applying the Pyramid in Real Projects

- **Emphasize Unit Tests**: Fast, reliable, and run on every commit.
- **Strengthen the API Layer**: Microservices demand robust contract testing.
- **Limit UI Tests**: Focus on a few key business-critical user journeys.

✗ Avoid the *inverted pyramid*—where 80% of tests are slow, brittle UI checks that fail for minor reasons.

Extend the Pyramid Thoughtfully

- **Performance Tests**: Run separately, not in every pipeline.
- **Security Tests**: OWASP ZAP or SonarQube in nightly builds.
- **Visual Tests**: Tools like Applitools or Percy to catch UI regressions.

Common Challenges & How to Mitigate

Every automation team runs into friction points, some technical, others organizational. Here's how to handle four of the most common ones:

Flaky UI Tests

You've probably seen them: tests that pass, then randomly fail the next run. This kind of unreliability is usually caused by unstable selectors or race conditions.

Fix it with:

➢ Smart, stable locators (e.g., data-test-id)
➢ Retry logic for intermittent failures
➢ The Page Object Model to isolate and reuse UI elements

⏱ Long Execution Times

Regression runs taking hours? That's a bottleneck you don't want in a CI/CD pipeline.

Fix it with:

> ➢ Parallel test execution (e.g., Pytest-xdist, JUnit5)
> ➢ Cloud-based test grids (e.g., Sauce Labs, BrowserStack)

🛠 High Maintenance Overhead

Automation that's hard to maintain quickly becomes shelfware. Poor naming, duplication, and brittle logic make your suite a burden.

Fix it with:

> ➢ Behavior-driven frameworks (Cucumber, SpecFlow)
> ➢ Clean, consistent naming conventions
> ➢ Git version control for auditability

♻ Test Duplication

Copy-pasting test logic leads to bloat and bugs.

Fix it with:

> ➢ Utility functions and reusable test modules
> ➢ Shared libraries for login flows, API auth, etc.

Pro Tip: Build your automation strategy like code: DRY (Don't Repeat Yourself), maintainable, and scalable by design.

Chapter Summary

Strategic automation isn't about doing more; it's about doing *smarter, and it* isn't "set it and forget it." It's a living system that evolves alongside your codebase. The most mature engineering teams aren't the ones with the most test cases; they're the ones who know **what not to automate**, and why.

☑ Chapter 3: Scandium System Software – A Modern Approach to Intelligent Test Automation

3.1 Introduction to Scandium Automation Testing

Scandium System Software is an end-to-end automation framework designed to eliminate testing bottlenecks, improve test coverage, and drive continuous quality at scale, from web interfaces to mobile apps and backend APIs. Whether implemented in a fintech platform, e-commerce system, or API-first architecture, Scandium offers a unified, extensible automation suite suitable for Agile and DevOps workflows. The Scandium framework represents a modern testing approach, prioritizing speed, intelligence, and modularity across various application domains.

3.2 Web Testing with Scandium

3.2.1 Overview

Web testing with Scandium accommodates the complexity of dynamic UIs, responsive designs, and cross-browser behavior. The automation engine supports functional validation, UI rendering, and compatibility testing, all underpinned by a modular architecture.

3.2.2 Key Features

- o Cross-Browser Execution: Compatible with Chrome, Firefox, Edge, and Safari
- o Headless Mode: Optimized for CI environments
- o Smart DOM Mapping: Reduces flakiness with adaptive element locators
- o Data-Driven Testing: Supports external data sources (CSV, JSON, Excel, APIs)
- o Visual Validation: Integrated pixel-based UI verification
- o Reusable Components: Encourages modular scripting and reusability

3.2.3 Real-Life Use Case:
E-commerce Checkout

Scandium automates the entire checkout process from login to payment gateway validation. It includes coupon validations, cart updates, and confirmation email triggers. Benefits over Manual Testing. Detects layout issues on different screen sizes automatically. Runs hundreds of test cases across browsers in minutes. Integrates with visual regression tools for pixel-perfect validation.

3.3 Mobile Testing with Scandium

3.3.1 Overview

Mobile automation in Scandium supports Android and iOS testing using both emulators and real devices. It addresses not only functional correctness, but also device-specific behavior such as gestures, location awareness, and performance profiling.

3.3.2 Key Features

- Native and Hybrid App Support
- Appium-based Core with proprietary extensions
- Gesture Simulation**: Swipe, pinch, drag, tap
- Battery and CPU Profiling
- Geo-location Simulation
- Biometric Emulation: Includes Face ID and fingerprint recognition

3.3.3 Real-Life Use Case:

Banking App Authentication

Scandium enabled automation of mobile banking scenarios, including:

- Secure login using biometrics, OTP delivery, and validation, Dashboard rendering verification, and Location-based feature validation. These automations supported 24/7 regression testing and earlier defect detection in staging environments.

3.4 API Testing with Scandium

3.4.1 Overview

Scandium's API testing engine is built for REST and GraphQL interfaces, emphasizing robustness and flexibility. It includes mock capabilities, schema validation, and request chaining.

3.4.2 Key Features

- o Request Chaining across multiple endpoints
- o Schema Validation using Swagger, OpenAPI, or GraphQL definitions
- o Authentication Support: OAuth2, JWT, Basic Auth
- o Contract Testing Integration (e.g., Pact-compatible)
- o Throttling and mocking of service responses
- o Load Simulation for service-level performance checks

3.4.3 Real-Life Use Case:

Healthcare Appointment System

API tests were developed to validate Patient record retrieval, Appointment creation and editing, Integration with insurance verification services, and Lab result submission workflows. The automation suite ensured test data consistency across environments and flagged schema changes before deployment, preventing regressions.

3.5 Why Scandium Outperforms Manual Testing

- o Although manual testing has merit in exploratory and UX evaluation, automated testing with Scandium provides several distinct advantages:
- o Repeatability across environments and releases
- o Execution Speed, especially in regression suites
- o Stability through smart element identification and script modularity
- o Collaboration between QA, development, and product teams
- o CI/CD Integration with platforms like Jenkins, GitHub Actions, and GitLab

Cost Reduction via lower test execution times and fewer manual cycles. Benchmarking showed that full regression cycles could be completed in 20 minutes, down from more than 5 hours, using Scandium automation pipelines.

3.6 Chapter Summary

Scandium System Software presents a full-spectrum automation framework for teams prioritizing speed, scalability, and quality assurance maturity. With dedicated support for Web, Mobile, and API testing, along with tight integration into modern DevOps toolchains, Scandium enables consistent, reliable, and maintainable testing practices. Its flexible design and feature depth make it a strong fit for organizations seeking high-value automation in real-world product delivery cycles.

Chapter 4: Choosing the Right Frameworks

Test automation is not just about writing scripts, it's about building a sustainable, scalable structure for those scripts to live in. That structure is your test automation framework. A well-chosen framework can improve code reusability, reduce maintenance costs, and foster collaboration between teams.

This chapter explores the three primary categories of automation frameworks: data-driven, keyword-driven, and hybrid, as well as complementary practices like BDD with Cucumber and the Page Object Model (POM) for UI automation.

4.1 Framework Types: Data-Driven, Keyword-Driven, and Hybrid

The choice of framework depends on your team's goals, skill set, application complexity, and test coverage needs. Each framework style comes with unique strengths and trade-offs.

4.1.1 Data-Driven Frameworks

A data-driven framework separates test data from test scripts. Test logic resides in reusable code, while data is stored externally (e.g., Excel, CSV, JSON, or databases).

☑ **Benefits:**

- High reusability: The same script can be run with multiple data sets.
- Simplified maintenance: Changes to test data don't require code updates.
- Better test coverage: Easily run the same test across various input scenarios.

⚠ **Challenges:**

- Requires building or integrating a robust data management layer.
- Slightly more technical complexity at setup.

Example: Testing a login form with 100 username/password combinations — a single script can loop through a spreadsheet instead of writing 100 separate test cases.

4.1.2 Keyword-Driven Frameworks

A keyword-driven framework uses high-level keywords to represent test actions (e.g., Click, EnterText, Verify). These keywords map to predefined functions or methods.

☑ **Benefits:**

- Enables collaboration: Business users or manual testers can write test scenarios using plain-language keywords.
- Reduces code duplication: Testers reuse keywords across multiple test cases.
- Improves test readability: Tests read like workflows or specifications.

⚠ **Challenges:**

- Requires a well-maintained keyword library.
- Less flexible for complex or highly customized logic.

Use Case: In a retail checkout test, a tester could write: Login → SearchProduct → AddToCart → Checkout using predefined keywords.

4.1.3 Hybrid Frameworks

A hybrid framework combines the strengths of both data-driven and keyword-driven models. It supports modularity, data abstraction, and readable workflows.

☑ Benefits:

- Highly customizable and adaptable to different testing needs.
- Balances technical depth and user accessibility.
- Supports layered architecture (utilities, business flows, data models).

⚠ Challenges:

- More complex to design and maintain.
- Requires team alignment on structure and naming conventions.

Hybrid frameworks are often the best choice for growing teams who need both flexibility and maintainability.

4.2 Behavior-Driven Development (BDD) with Cucumber

Behavior-Driven Development (BDD) is a collaborative approach that brings together developers, testers, and product owners to define test scenarios in a shared language. Cucumber is a popular tool that supports BDD using the Gherkin syntax.

4.2.1 Key BDD Concepts

Feature files: Written in plain English to describe application behavior.

Scenarios: Specific user stories or use cases.

Step definitions: Glue code that connects Gherkin steps to automation scripts.

Example Gherkin Scenario:

```pgsql
Feature: Login
Scenario: Successful Login
Given the user is on the login page
When the user enters valid credentials
Then they should be redirected to the dashboard
```

4.2.2 Benefits of BDD with Cucumber

- Improves collaboration between QA, developers, and business stakeholders.
- Bridges the gap between requirements and test scripts.
- Encourages living documentation: feature files double as specs and tests.

BDD works well in Agile teams, where communication and shared understanding are key.

4.3 Page Object Model (POM) for UI Test Automation

The Page Object Model (POM) design pattern enhances UI test automation by separating test logic from the web page structure.

4.3.1 Key Concepts

Page Object: A class representing a specific web page (or section).

Page Methods: Functions that define user actions on that page.

For example, a LoginPage class might contain methods like **enterUsername()**, **enterPassword()**, and **clickLogin().**

4.3.2 Benefits of POM

- Reduces code duplication by encapsulating UI logic in reusable objects.
- Simplifies maintenance: if the UI changes, you only update the Page Object.
- Improves readability: test scripts call descriptive methods instead of raw selectors.

Pro Tip: Pair POM with a Base Page class for common actions like clicking buttons, waiting for elements, or handling alerts.

📋 CHAPTER SUMMARY

Choosing the right framework means balancing reusability, maintainability, and readability. In smaller teams, data-driven frameworks might be enough. In larger, cross-functional teams, hybrid frameworks with BDD and POM offer better long-term value.

"A good test automation framework doesn't just make testing easier — it makes collaboration, scalability, and refactoring easier too."

✍ Chapter 5: Tooling for Test Automation

Choosing the right tools isn't just about features, it's about fit, flexibility, and futureproofing.

5.1 Open-Source vs. Commercial Tools

When it comes to test automation, tooling is often where teams get stuck. There's no shortage of options from powerful open-source platforms to slick commercial suites. But choosing tools based only on popularity or price can lead to mismatched capabilities, underutilization, or vendor lock-in.

Let's break down the two main categories: open-source and commercial tools.

5.1.1 Open-Source Tools

Open-source test automation tools are free and typically developed by passionate global communities. They offer flexibility, customization, and continuous innovation; often outpacing their commercial counterparts in niche capabilities.

Advantages:

- **Cost-effective:** No licensing fees, which makes them ideal for startups and small teams.
- **Customizable:** You can tailor the framework to match your app architecture or workflow.
- **Community-driven:** Large ecosystems mean access to plugins, integrations, and support forums.

Disadvantages:

- **Lack of formal support:** When things break, your team is the support team.
- **Maintenance-intensive:** You often need in-house scripting and DevOps expertise to build and maintain pipelines.

Example: Selenium WebDriver is powerful but requires developers to build their frameworks and reporting systems around it.

5.1.2 Commercial Tools

Commercial tools are backed by companies that offer dedicated support, enterprise features, and plug-and-play capabilities. These are attractive to teams who need speed, stability, and integrated dashboards out of the box.

Advantages:

- **Official support and documentation:** Peace of mind when dealing with bugs or blockers.
- **Faster onboarding:** GUIs, low-code editors, and built-in templates reduce ramp-up time.
- **Integrated features:** Reporting, test management, CI/CD hooks are often included.

⚠ Disadvantages:

- **Cost:** Licensing fees can be steep, especially as your test volume grows.
- **Customization limitations:** You may be locked into how the tool is designed to work.

🔵 **Pro Insight:** For regulated industries (e.g., finance, healthcare), commercial tools can provide built-in compliance, audit trails, and risk-based test prioritization.

5.2 Web Automation Tools: Selenium, Cypress, and Playwright

Web testing remains one of the most common areas for automation, and three tools dominate the space: Selenium, Cypress, and Playwright.

5.2.1 Selenium

Selenium is the veteran of web automation, a robust open-source tool that supports multiple languages and browsers.

Key Features:

- **Language support**: supports multiple programming languages such as Java, Python, C#, Ruby, JavaScript
- **Browser coverage:** Chrome, Firefox, Safari, Edge, IE
- Test grid support for parallel execution

☑ **Pros:**

- Highly customizable
- Massive ecosystem and community
- Works across most platforms and browsers

⚠ **Cons:**

- Steep learning curve
- Requires custom-built frameworks and reporting tools
- Slower execution speed compared to newer tools

➕ Best for: Teams that need deep customization and already have engineering support for test infra.

5.2.2 Cypress

Cypress is a modern testing framework that runs in the browser, offering fast and developer-friendly automation.

Key Features:

- JavaScript-based
- Built-in test runner and dashboard
- Time travel and real-time debugging

Pros:

- Super-fast and stable test runs
- Great for front-end teams (especially React/Vue)
- Simplified setup, no drivers or server layers

Cons:

- Limited cross-browser support (no Safari, IE in early versions)
- No native multi-tab or multi-origin support (now improving)
- JS-only (though TypeScript is supported)

Best for: Frontend teams, startups, and TDD/Agile squads looking for speed and simplicity.

5.2.3 Playwright

Playwright, developed by Microsoft, is a powerful open-source tool offering cross-browser and cross-language capabilities with high reliability.

Key Features:

- Supports JavaScript, Python, Java, and .NET
- Automates Chrome, Firefox, Safari with one API
- Headless and headful modes

Pros:

- Multi-browser + multi-language support
- Robust API testing, file uploads, downloads, and shadow DOM support
- Test isolation with built-in context and browser management

Cons:

- Still newer than Selenium (but maturing rapidly)
- Slightly heavier to install than Cypress

Best for: Teams needing broad browser coverage and deep automation features in CI/CD pipelines.

5.3 Appium for Mobile Testing

Appium is the go-to tool for mobile test automation across Android and iOS. It's open-source and works by wrapping native frameworks like XCUITest and Espresso.

Key Features:

- Supports hybrid, native, and mobile web apps
- Language support: Java, Python, JavaScript, C#
- Works with emulators and real devices

Pros:

- Cross-platform support
- Large, active open-source community
- Compatible with Selenium WebDriver

Cons:

- Setup can be complex (esp. for iOS)
- Slower test execution compared to desktop tools

Pro Tip: Pair Appium with services like Sauce Labs or BrowserStack to run mobile tests on real cloud devices.

5.4 API Testing Tools: Postman and RestAssured

APIs are the glue of modern applications; testing them early and thoroughly is essential.

5.4.1 Postman

Postman is a GUI-based API testing platform, widely used for manual, exploratory, and automated API testing.

Pros:

- Easy to learn
- Great for exploratory testing and documentation
- Supports test scripts via JavaScript

Cons:

- Can be costly
- Less suited for large-scale regression automation

5.4.2 RestAssured

RestAssured is a Java-based open-source framework built for automated REST API testing.

Pros:

- Full Java support with fluent syntax
- Easily integrated into Maven or Gradle projects
- Ideal for API test automation in CI/CD
- Cost-effectiveness

Cons:

- Java-only (not as accessible for non-devs)
- Requires coding knowledge

Recommendation: Use Postman for collaboration and onboarding, and RestAssured for long-term automated API pipelines.

5.5 Scandium System (Custom or Composite Framework)

Scandium appears to be a custom or proprietary platform mentioned across chapters for testing APIs, web interfaces, CI/CD integration, and email flows.

If you're designing or advocating Scandium, here's how to position it:

Features:

- Unified support for API, Web UI, email, and CI/CD
- Data-driven and functional test support
- Supports integrations and reporting pipelines

Pros:

- Centralized test management
- Promotes team collaboration
- Customizable for internal systems

Cons:

- May lack third-party community support
- Requires dedicated internal expertise to maintain

Positioning Tip: Present Scandium as a scalable internal test platform that combines the strengths of open-source tooling under a unified architecture.

📖 Chapter 6: Industry-Specific Test Automation Approaches

There's no one-size-fits-all in test automation; context is everything.

Test automation must adapt to the domain it serves. What works well for a media startup may not apply in healthcare, fintech, or e-commerce. Each industry carries unique workflows, compliance requirements, and system complexities, and that means the automation approach must evolve accordingly.

This chapter explores how automation strategies should be customized across common industries: healthcare, finance, e-commerce, logistics, and telecommunications.

6.1 Automation in Healthcare

Healthcare applications require a deep focus on data integrity, compliance, and patient safety. Whether it's an EMR (Electronic Medical Records) system or a telemedicine platform, the failure cost is high, putting test automation in a mission-critical role.

- **Key Challenges:**
    - Ensuring the security and confidentiality of patient data
    - Meeting strict regulatory compliance requirements
    - Complex systems with multiple integrations
- **Test Automation Benefits:**
    - Improved security and confidentiality of patient data
    - Enhanced compliance with regulatory requirements
    - Faster time-to-market for new healthcare products and services
- **Examples of Test Automation in Healthcare:**
    - Automated testing of electronic health records (EHRs) systems
    - Testing of medical imaging and diagnostic systems
    - Automation of compliance testing for HIPAA (Health Insurance Portability and Accountability Act) and other regulatory requirements

Key Considerations:

- HIPAA and data privacy laws (e.g., anonymization, access control)
- Audit trails: Ensure test frameworks can log all test actions for traceability
- Test data masking: Never use real patient data in test environments
- System integration: Test interoperability across labs, pharmacies, insurance databases, etc.

🧠 **Practical Tip:** Use synthetic data generators and containerized databases to test workflows without compromising compliance.

6.2 Automation in Finance and Fintech

In financial systems, even a one-second outage or a misplaced decimal can lead to massive losses. Security, auditability, and transactional consistency are nonnegotiable. Test automation plays a crucial role in ensuring the reliability, security, and performance of these systems.

🔍 Key Priorities:

- Regression automation: Particularly around critical transaction flows
- Security testing: Automated vulnerability scanning (e.g., OWASP ZAP)
- Compliance checks: Ensure workflows follow PCI-DSS or SOX guidelines
- Load testing: Validate system behavior during peak hours (e.g., market opening)

Key Challenges:

- High risk of financial loss due to system failures
- Strict regulatory compliance requirements
- Complex systems with multiple integrations

Test Automation Benefits:

- Improved accuracy and reliability of financial transactions
- Enhanced security and compliance with regulatory requirements
- Faster time-to-market for new products and services

Examples of Test Automation in Finance and Banking:

- Automated testing of online banking and mobile banking applications
- Testing of payment processing systems and gateways
- Automation of compliance testing for anti-money laundering (AML) and know-your-customer (KYC) regulations.

🏛 Example: In banking apps, automation must validate not only UI elements but also real-time balance updates, latency, and retry mechanisms.

6.3 Automation in E-commerce

E-commerce platforms handle constant feature releases, dynamic UIs, and a wide variety of user interactions, from search to checkout.

Key Testing Areas:

- Cross-browser/UI testing: Products and carts must behave consistently across devices
- API contract tests: Especially for inventory, payments, and user profiles
- Performance tests: Black Friday or flash sales require load-tested backends
- Visual testing: Minor CSS bugs can disrupt pricing displays and conversions

6.4 Automation in Logistics and Supply Chain Systems

Logistics platforms often span inventory, fleet management, real-time tracking, and warehouse automation. These are deeply integration-heavy systems, where a breakdown in one service affects many others.

Focus Areas:

- End-to-end test flows: From order creation to delivery tracking
- Device simulation: Automate GPS, RFID, and sensor data streams
- Data sync checks: Between ERP systems and tracking dashboards
- Asynchronous workflow testing: Test systems that rely on background queues and messaging

Realistic Scenario: Use API mocks and timeouts to simulate delayed shipments, reroutes, or cancellations, and validate fallback logic.

6.5 Automation in Telecommunications

Telco platforms involve high-throughput, concurrent systems, often dealing with real-time charging, billing, SIM activations, and network service provisioning.

Test Strategy Essentials:

- Concurrency and thread testing: Simulate high-volume operations (e.g., activating 5,000 lines)
- Legacy integrations: Many telcos still rely on legacy platforms — automation must bridge SOAP, mainframes, and REST APIs
- Service virtualization: Use tools like WireMock to simulate network behavior
- Time-based tests: Handle scheduled plan renewals, billing cycles, and latency thresholds

Pro Tip: For systems like mobile recharge or postpaid billing, ensure automation validates workflows across both frontend and backend systems (e.g., charging rules, tax calculations, etc.).

6.6 Shared Patterns Across Industries

Regardless of industry, some best practices apply everywhere:

Best Practice	Why It Matters
Test Data Isolation	Prevents one test case from corrupting another
CI/CD Integration	Enables faster feedback and continuous testing

Environment Parity	Mirror production as closely as possible
Risk-Based-Test Prioritization	Helps decide what to automate first (based on business risk)
Security-First Approach	Security is everyone's job. Automate vulnerability scans

How to Tailor Frameworks to Industries

While the core architecture of your automation framework may remain constant (e.g., hybrid or POM-based), certain modules or plugins will differ depending on the domain.

Industry	Special Plugins/Approach
Healthcare	Test data masking, audit trail loggers
Finance	Transaction validator modules, SOX compliance hooks
E-commerce	Visual testing plugins, geolocation handling
Logistics	API mocking for real-time sensors
Telecom	Parallel test runners, event simulation tools

Framework Tip: Keep your framework modular to plug in domain-specific components without reinventing the core.

Chapter 7: Integrating Automation into CI/CD Pipelines

7.0 Introduction

"If it's not tested continuously, it's not ready for production."

As modern development processes continue to evolve, Continuous Integration (CI) and Continuous Delivery/Deployment (CD) have become critical to rapid, high-quality software delivery. CI/CD provides the foundation for teams to release code frequently and reliably. However, these pipelines are only as effective as the quality of testing integrated into them.

This chapter explores how automation fits into the CI/CD lifecycle, tools that support these processes, and best practices for integrating automation meaningfully into your pipelines.

7.1 Understanding CI/CD in Context

What is CI?

Continuous Integration (CI) is the practice of merging code into a shared repository several times a day. Each merge triggers a set of automated tasks, typically unit tests, static code analysis, and builds, to verify that changes don't break the existing system.

What is CD?

Continuous Delivery (CD) extends CI by automating the delivery process, pushing code to a staging environment for further validation. Continuous Deployment goes one step further: code that passes all checks is automatically released to production — no manual intervention required.

🔧 In a mature DevOps pipeline, CI/CD ensures code is built, tested, and delivered reliably, with automation at every stage.

7.2 The Role of Test Automation in CI/CD

Test automation is central to the success of a CI/CD pipeline. Without it, teams risk releasing buggy, untested, or insecure code to production. By embedding automation at every phase, from unit tests on commit to post-deployment monitoring, teams create a self-validating system that promotes stability and scalability.

Core Purposes:

* ❖ Early bug detection
* ❖ Faster feedback loops
* ❖ Lower deployment risk
* ❖ Standardized validation across teams and environments

7.3 Key Features of Automation in CI/CD

Features and Description

Version Control Integration: Code triggers automation via Git events (push, PR, merge)

Environment Consistency: Use Docker/Kubernetes to standardize test environments

Parallel Execution: Run tests across browsers, APIs, and devices simultaneously

Failure Notifications: Integrate Slack, Teams, or email alerts for failed pipelines

Test Reporting: Generate real-time dashboards (e.g., Allure, ReportPortal)

Best pipelines fail fast, provide traceable logs, and surface flaky tests before production does.

7.4 CI/CD Automation Flow

Here's a typical flow integrating test automation into a CI/CD pipeline:

1. Developer pushes code → GitHub/GitLab repo
2. CI pipeline triggers → Build + Unit tests run
3. Static analysis & linting → Code quality checks
4. Integration tests → API & service layer validation
5. UI tests → Selenium/Cypress tests validate the frontend
6. Deployment to staging
7. Performance & Security scans
8. Manual approval or auto-deploy to production

7.5 Benefits of Integrating Automation into CI/CD

❖ **Faster Time-to-Market:** Automation reduces manual intervention, streamlining the release process.
❖ **Improved Software Quality:** Automated tests catch regressions and edge cases early.
❖ **Consistency and Repeatability**: CI/CD ensures that builds are tested under consistent conditions.
❖ **Increased Team Collaboration:** Developers, testers, and DevOps engineers align around automated pipelines.
❖ **Early Detection of Defects**: Failures are caught before they reach production, reducing costly rollbacks.

A strong CI/CD pipeline turns deployment from a risky event into a routine operation.

7.5 Tools Supporting CI/CD Testing

The following tools are commonly used in modern pipelines to support continuous testing:

➢ Jenkins
➢ GitHub Actions
➢ GitLab CI/CD
➢ CircleCI
➢ Azure DevOps
➢ Bitbucket Pipelines

Each of these tools plays a unique role depending on project requirements, team preferences, and integration needs.

7.5.1 Jenkins

Jenkins is an open-source automation server that enables developers to build, test, and deploy code automatically. It is one of the most widely adopted CI tools in the industry.

Key Features:

➢ Plugin-based architecture
➢ Supports scripting (Groovy, Shell, Python)
➢ Scalable via agent nodes (master-slave architecture)
➢ Integrates with Git, Maven, Docker, Selenium, etc.

Implementation Steps:

➢ Install Jenkins on a local or cloud server.
➢ Configure your build environment and install relevant plugins (e.g., Git, Allure, Docker).
➢ Define a Jenkinsfile to script your pipeline using stages (build → test → deploy).
➢ Connect your code repository (e.g., GitHub).
➢ Trigger builds automatically via webhooks or scheduled jobs (cron).

Jenkins is ideal for teams needing flexibility and deep customization.

7.5.2 GitHub Actions

GitHub Actions allows developers to automate workflows directly in their GitHub repositories using YAML-based definitions.

Key Features:

➢ Native GitHub integration
➢ Fast setup using .github/workflows/*.yml files
➢ Built-in actions marketplace
➢ Supports container-based builds and matrix testing

Implementation Steps:

- ➢ Create a .yml workflow file in .github/workflows/.
- ➢ Define the trigger (on: push, on: pull_request, etc.).
- ➢ Add jobs with steps: checkout code → install dependencies → run tests → deploy.
- ➢ Use secrets and environment variables to secure tokens and credentials.

Best for teams already using GitHub and looking for tight integration with minimal setup overhead.

7.5.3 GitLab CI/CD

GitLab's built-in CI/CD tool is one of the most comprehensive in the DevOps space.

Key Features:

- ➢ Fully integrated with Git repositories
- ➢ Supports multiple programming languages and frameworks
- ➢ Built-in Docker support
- ➢ Pipeline visualization, environment-specific deployments

Implementation Steps:

- ➢ Create a .gitlab-ci.yml file at the root of your repo.
- ➢ Define stages: build, test, deploy.
- ➢ Assign each job to a runner (shared or self-hosted).
- ➢ Configure pipelines via GitLab UI and track build/test history.

GitLab CI/CD is perfect for self-managed or end-to-end DevOps pipelines.

7.5.4 CircleCI

CircleCI is a modern CI/CD tool known for its speed, container-native approach, and developer-friendliness.

Key Features:

- ➢ Parallel test execution
- ➢ Built-in caching
- ➢ First-class Docker support
- ➢ Configured via .circleci/config.yml

Implementation Steps:

- ➢ Create a CircleCI account and link your GitHub/GitLab repo.
- ➢ Add a config.yml file inside a .circleci/ directory.
- ➢ Define workflows and jobs: checkout → test → deploy.
- ➢ Use orbs (reusable packages) to simplify configuration.

CircleCI is a great fit for fast-moving dev teams working with containers and microservices.

7.5.5 Azure DevOps

Azure DevOps provides a suite of development tools, including Azure Pipelines, which supports both CI/CD.

Key Features:

> YAML or GUI-based pipeline configuration
> Full integration with the Microsoft ecosystem
> Test plans and reporting
> Supports GitHub, Bitbucket, and Azure Repos

Implementation Steps:

> Set up a pipeline using the Azure DevOps UI or azure-pipelines.yml.
> Define triggers and link to your repo.
> Add pipeline tasks: restore → build → test → publish artifacts → deploy.
> Use environments and approvals for stage control.

Best suited for enterprise teams, especially those using .NET, Azure Cloud, or Microsoft services.

7.5.6 Bitbucket Pipelines

Bitbucket Pipelines offers integrated CI/CD capabilities for Bitbucket repositories.

Key Features:

> YAML configuration
> Native integration with Bitbucket
> Lightweight, quick setup
> Docker support and caching

Implementation Steps:

> Add a bitbucket-pipelines.yml file at the root of your repo.
> Define pipelines and steps for your stages.
> Use deployment environments and variables securely.
> Monitor builds and deployments from the Bitbucket UI.

Best for Atlassian-based teams already using Bitbucket + Jira.

Pro Tip: Choose tools that support your language stack, cloud provider, and team workflow.

7.6 Common Challenges and Solutions

Challenge	Mitigation Strategy
Flaky Tests	Use smart locators, retry logic, and test isolation
Long Execution Times	Implement parallel testing, caching, and test filtering

Environment Inconsistency	Use Docker containers for parity
Poor Visibility into Failures	Integrate dashboards and use real-time alerts

7.7 Version Control Strategies for Test Automation

Version control is essential for managing test automation code and ensuring collaboration among team members.

- **Key Strategies:**
    - Use a version control system (e.g., Git, SVN) to manage test automation code
    - Create separate branches for test automation code and application code
    - Use a consistent naming convention for test automation code and files
    - Implement a code review process for test automation code changes

By integrating automated tests with CI/CD pipelines and implementing effective version control strategies, teams can ensure that their test automation efforts are efficient, reliable, and scalable.

☑ Chapter 8: Performance Testing in Test Automation

8.0 Introduction

In modern digital systems, performance is no longer a luxury, it's a baseline expectation. Users demand instant responses, seamless transactions, and zero tolerance for lag. Performance testing is essential in ensuring that applications can scale and deliver reliable user experiences under real-world load conditions. While functional testing verifies if features work as expected, performance testing determines how well the system responds under pressure, and whether it breaks when usage spikes. This chapter provides a practical approach to embedding performance testing in modern test automation pipelines, using real tools, examples, and metrics relevant to today's DevOps and Agile environments.

8.1 The Role of Performance Testing in Automation

Automated performance testing allows QA and DevOps teams to:

- Continuously measure system speed and responsiveness.
- Detect bottlenecks early in the development lifecycle.
- Validate how systems behave under load, over time, or under failure conditions. Track degradation, scalability, and regression in performance.

In CI/CD, performance testing isn't a one-time activity; it's part of a living, repeatable system.

8.2 Benefits of Automated Performance Testing

- o Speed and Efficiency: Automate thousands of user interactions without manual effort.
- o Scalability: Simulate traffic patterns to stress-test APIs, UIs, or databases.
- o Early Bottleneck Detection: Identify failures before release.
- o Real-time Metrics: Monitor response times, error rates, and resource usage instantly.
- o Integration with CI/CD: Embed performance validation directly into pipelines.

8.3 Common Types of Performance Tests

Test Type and Description

- ❖ **Load Testing**: Simulates expected user traffic to assess performance under normal conditions.
- ❖ **Stress Testing:** Pushes the system beyond its limits to observe failure behavior.
- ❖ **Spike Testing:** Introduces sudden traffic spikes to evaluate responsiveness.
- ❖ **Endurance (Soak) Testing:** Evaluates how the system performs over an extended period.
- ❖ **Scalability Testing:** Determines how well a system adapts to increased workload or resources.

- ❖ **Volume Testing:** Checks system performance with large data volumes.

- Run load tests early. Stress and soak tests are best reserved for staging or pre-production.

8.4 Tools for Performance Testing

8.4.1 Apache JMeter

Key Features:

- ❖ Open-source, GUI + CLI interface.
- ❖ Supports Web, REST, SOAP, FTP, JDBC, etc.
- ❖ Rich plugin ecosystem.
- ❖ Data parameterization, assertions, and listener support.

Use Case: Simulate 1,000 users logging into a banking platform and querying account history. Test results are exported to Jenkins for pass/fail evaluation based on response time thresholds.

8.4.2 Gatling

Key Features:

- ❖ Scala-based DSL for scripting
- ❖ HTML reports with detailed metrics
- ❖ Integrates easily into CI/CD pipelines (Jenkins, GitLab, Maven).
- ❖ Lightweight and fast execution

Use Case: An API gateway is tested with 10,000 requests/minute using Gatling scripts written by developers. The build fails if the P95 response time exceeds 450ms.

8.4.3 k6 (by Grafana Labs)

Key Features:

- ❖ JavaScript scripting engine
- ❖ Threshold checks for automated test validation.
- ❖ Cloud and CLI execution
- ❖ Real-time reporting into Grafana dashboards

Use Case: A retail checkout process is tested nightly in pre-prod using `k6`. Results are pushed to Grafana dashboards for performance monitoring and trend analysis.

8.4.4 LoadRunner (Micro Focus)

Key Features:

- ❖ Enterprise-grade platform supporting SAP, Citrix, and Oracle.
- ❖ Full test lifecycle management
- ❖ Visual analysis dashboards.
- ❖ Supports legacy systems and modern cloud apps

⚙ **Use Case:** An insurance company tests its claims system with LoadRunner, validating that it handles 5,000 concurrent agents processing records during peak hours.

8.5 Key Metrics to Track

❖ **Average Response Time:** The time it takes for a typical request to complete.
❖ **Latency (P90, P95, P99):** How the slowest users are experiencing the system.
❖ Throughput Requests or transactions per second.
❖ **Error Rate:** The percentage of requests that fail under load.
❖ **Resource Usage:** CPU, memory, and disk usage under stress.
❖ **Time to First Byte (TTFB):** How quickly the server starts to respond.

📊 Insight: Always track percentiles, they reveal degradation that averages often hide.

8.6 Integrating Performance Testing into CI/CD Pipelines

To automate performance testing effectively:

i.   Embed "smoke load tests" after unit and integration stages.
ii. Use "thresholds*" to fail builds if performance degrades (e.g., > 300ms P95).
iii. Schedule "full load or soak tests" as part of nightly builds.
iv. Integrate "metrics and results" into Grafana, InfluxDB, or other dashboards.
v.   Use "cloud-based testing platforms" for distributed, large-scale simulations.

Typical flow:

1. Developer commits → CI triggers
2. Unit + functional tests run
3. k6 or JMeter runs a smoke load test
4. Performance gates evaluate thresholds 5. Results visualized or logged for trend tracking.

8.7 Common Challenges and How to Overcome Them

➤ User Scenarios: Use analytics or logs to build test flows
➤ No historical trend tracking: Store performance metrics in time-series DBs (e.g., InfluxDB)
➤ Long test execution time: Isolate smoke tests and schedule heavier tests separately
➤ Poor Visualization: Export metrics to Prometheus or Grafana
➤ Inconsistent Results: Warm-up services before actual tests

💡 Tip: Performance issues are often data-dependent. Don't forget to vary inputs and test with real-world payload sizes

8.8 Chapter Summary

Performance testing ensures your application doesn't just function, it performs reliably at scale. Automated performance testing empowers teams to release confidently, knowing that load, latency, and system degradation are under control. The key is continuous performance awareness, not one-off validation. Start small, automate early, test what matters most, and scale when ready. Don't wait until your app hits production to find out it's too slow.

Chapter 9: AI and Machine Learning in Test Automation

9.0 Introduction

Artificial Intelligence (AI) and Machine Learning (ML) are reshaping the future of software testing. In a world of increasing software complexity and rapid delivery cycles, the ability to intelligently automate tests and even allow tests to adapt autonomously is becoming a game-changer. This chapter focuses on two key applications of AI in test automation: Self-healing tests that fix themselves when things break and AI-powered test generation and maintenance that learns from data and changes in the system. We'll explore how these capabilities work, their benefits, the tools implementing them, and how to responsibly use AI in testing real-world applications.

9.1 Self-Healing Test Automation

9.1.1 What is Self-Healing Automation?

Self-healing automation refers to the ability of an automated test system to detect and repair test failures caused by UI changes such as updates to element locators, CSS classes, or layout shifts, without human intervention. Instead of breaking when a button's `id` changes from `submit-btn` to `submit-payment`, the test dynamically adapts by using alternate locator strategies like text, relative position, or AI models trained on previous UI states.

Self-healing tests save hundreds of hours by eliminating tedious locator fixes after every UI change.

9.1.2 How Does It Work?

AI/ML algorithms monitor test execution and locate failing elements. The system uses **historical test data** and **DOM structure analysis** to re-map locators. Some tools use **confidence scoring** to pick the most likely matching element. Updated locators are automatically stored or suggested to the user for approval

9.1.3 Tools Supporting Self-Healing

- ➢ **Testim**: Uses AI to auto-correct element selectors.
- ➢ **Mabl**: Detects DOM changes and adjusts tests accordingly.
- ➢ **Functionize:** Learns UI structure to suggest smart fallback locators.
- ➢ **Katalon Studio (Smart Wait):** Uses object properties to dynamically re-identify elements.

9.1.4 Benefits of Self-Healing Tests

- ➢ Reduced Maintenance Overhead: Less time fixing brittle UI scripts
- ➢ Increased Test Stability: Tests fail less due to minor UI changes
  Faster Feedback Loops: Less debugging and manual reruns
  Enhanced Resilience: Tests keep running even when elements are renamed or moved

9.2 AI-Powered Test Generation and Maintenance

AI isn't just helping fix tests, it's now generating them.

9.2.1 What Is It?

AI-powered test generation refers to systems that automatically create new tests or optimize existing ones using:

- ➢ Code analysis
- ➢ User behavior modeling
- ➢ Production telemetry
- ➢ Test result trends

These systems apply natural language processing (NLP), predictive modeling, and pattern recognition to determine what needs to be tested and how.

9.2.2 How It Works

Machine learning models review application code, UI changes, or logs. AI identifies untested paths, risky areas, or regressions. The system creates new test cases or updates old ones based on these insights. Some tools run test impact analysis to select only the tests relevant to a given change.

9.2.3 Tools Offering This Capability

- ➢ Testim: Uses AI for both test creation and maintenance.
- ➢ Mabl: Generates UI flows automatically and adapts them based on page evolution.
- ➢ AutonomIQ (by Sauce Labs): Generates tests from natural language or requirements.
- ➢ Diffblue Cover: AI unit test generation tool for Java.
- ➢ Launchable: Predicts which tests to run based on recent code changes and historical failures.

9.2.4 Benefits of AI-Generated Testing

- ➢ Broader Test Coverage: AI can test combinations that humans may overlook.
- ➢ Faster Test Development: Reduces the manual effort of writing test cases.
- ➢ Risk-Based Prioritization: Focus on high-risk areas based on data.
- ➢ Test Optimization: Avoid running unnecessary or low-impact tests.

9.3 Use Cases in Real-World Teams

- ➢ E-commerce: Self-healing tests automatically update element locators during A/B experiments.
- ➢ Banking apps: Test impact analysis helps prioritize testing for critical transaction flows.
- ➢ Agile startups: Use AI-generated smoke tests from UI behavior to accelerate sprint feedback.

🌐 Even if teams don't go fully AI-native, combining AI with traditional automation can significantly boost productivity and reduce flakiness.

9.4 Ethical Considerations in AI Testing

As AI becomes more autonomous in testing and decision-making, ethics must be part of the conversation.

Risks:

- ➤ False confidence: AI-generated tests may miss business logic if unchecked.
- ➤ Bias: Algorithms trained on limited datasets may reinforce edge-case blind spots.
- ➤ Accountability: Who is responsible if a bug slips through AI validation?

Best Practices:

- ➤ Always review AI-generated scripts before production use.
- ➤ Include human-in-the-loop validation where critical decisions are made.
- ➤ Monitor for model drift or misbehavior in AI-powered components.

9.5 Limitations of AI in Test Automation

- o Cannot fully replace human intuition and exploratory testing
- o May generate noisy or irrelevant tests without good training data
- o Requires initial investment in tools, training, and workflow integration
- o Debugging AI-driven tests can be non-transparent ("black box" logic)

✦ AI is a powerful augmentation, not a replacement, at least for now.

9.6 Chapter Summary

AI and machine learning are dramatically transforming test automation, from healing broken scripts to autonomously generating tests based on application data. While these tools offer enormous promise in boosting coverage, reducing maintenance, and enabling smarter test selection, they are not silver bullets. Teams should combine the strengths of AI with human expertise, ethical oversight, and strategic implementation. By doing so, testing becomes not only smarter but also more scalable and future-proof.

☑ Chapter 10: Best Practices for Maintaining Automation Code

10.0 Introduction

Automation is never a "write-once, forget-forever" investment. As applications evolve, automated test suites must be continuously maintained to remain effective. Even the most robust test suites will require maintenance, especially in Agile and DevOps environments where changes happen fast. Poorly maintained automation leads to broken tests, increased flakiness, wasted time spent on debugging and reruns, and eventually, loss of trust in the system. Well-maintained tests, on the other hand, provide fast, reliable feedback and inspire confidence in release quality.

🔍 Think of test maintenance as gardening; it's not glamorous, but without it, everything falls apart.

This chapter focuses on two critical areas:

1. Managing flaky tests, those that fail intermittently without a valid cause
2. Refactoring and optimizing test scripts to ensure long-term maintainability

10.1 Managing Flaky Tests

Flaky tests are one of the most frustrating aspects of test automation. They often pass locally but fail in CI environments or fail randomly across runs with no changes in code. These tests not only slow down the development process, but they also erode confidence in the entire automation suite through reruns and false debugging. They hide real bugs by causing test noise.

10.1.1 Identify and Isolate Flaky Tests

Use the following techniques to detect flaky behavior:

- o Test Analytics Tools: Platforms like Allure TestOps, CircleCI Insights, or Buildkite Analytics help track test pass/fail trends across time.
- o Retry and Logging: Temporarily enable retries with verbose logging to isolate patterns.
- o Tag or Quarantine: Label flaky tests (`@flaky`) and isolate them from the core test suite.

Pro Tip: Automate the detection of flakiness. Tests that fail inconsistently across 3+ runs should be flagged for review.

10.1.2 Common Causes of Flaky Tests

- o UI Changes: Small DOM shifts or locator changes cause UI tests to break even when functionality is fine.
- o Dynamic Content or Timing Issues: Elements that appear asynchronously (e.g., loading spinners, animations) can throw off static waits.
- o Test Data Dependencies: Hardcoded or reused data can cause conflicts across runs (e.g., duplicate usernames or expired sessions).

- Third-Party Service Failures: APIs, payment gateways, or integrations that become temporarily unavailable can cause test failures unrelated to the app.
- Environment Instability: Differences between local, staging, or CI environments (timeouts, response times) often trigger inconsistencies.

10.1.3 Fixing Flaky Tests

- Use explicit waits or synchronization techniques (`WebDriverWait`, `cy.waitUntil()`).
- Avoid hardcoding test data, use factories, mock APIs, or DB reset scripts.
- Refactor tests to make them atomic, one test, one outcome.
- Use page object models to isolate and improve selector reliability.
- If needed, add limited retry logic (e.g., retry 2 times, then fail definitively).

⚠ Warning: Avoid hiding real issues with blind retries. Fix the root cause first.

10.2 Refactoring and Optimizing Automation Scripts

Maintaining a clean, efficient automation codebase is just as important as writing functional tests. As projects grow, unoptimized or duplicated code becomes a long-term liability.

10.2.1 Refactoring Strategies

- Simplify and improve test scripts using these techniques:
- DRY Principle: Eliminate duplicated code. Use reusable methods or shared utilities.
- Improve Readability: Use meaningful names, comments, and concise logic.
- Break Down Large Tests: Modularize long workflows into reusable steps.
- Use Page Object Models: Centralize selectors and actions for maintainability. Example Before: ```python driver.find_element_by_xpath("//div[2]/button[1]").click() ``` Example After: ```python loginPage.clickLoginButton() ```

10.2.2 Optimization Techniques

Optimizing test suites reduces execution time and infrastructure costs.

- Parallel Execution: Run tests concurrently using tools like TestNG, PyTest-xdist, or cloud grids like BrowserStack.
- Smart Test Selection: Run only impacted tests (via tools like Launchable).
- Test Data Strategy: Use mock data, shared fixtures, and isolated test accounts.
- Intelligent Waits: Replace static waits (`Thread.sleep()`) with condition-based waits.
- Caching: Avoid repeating costly operations (e.g., login for each test).

 Tip: Run long regression tests in nightly builds. Keep PR pipelines fast with tagged smoke or critical-path tests.

10.3 Real-World Example

A startup noticed its test suite time ballooned from 8 minutes to 30 as new features were added. Upon investigation, they discovered redundant test steps across 15 test cases and several flaky assertions. By refactoring common flows into shared methods, introducing page objects, and marking flaky tests for review, they reduced execution time by 40% and cut CI pipeline failures by half.

10.4 Chapter Summary

Test maintenance is not a cost, it's an investment. Flaky tests can cripple release confidence, and bloated test code slows delivery. Teams that actively refactor, optimize, and stabilize their test suites see massive returns in developer trust, delivery speed, and software quality. The goal of automation is not just coverage, it's sustainable, scalable, and valuable testing over time.

Chapter 11: Future Trends and Emerging Technologies in Test Automation

11.0 Introduction

The field of test automation is undergoing a seismic shift. Driven by technologies like artificial intelligence, low-code development, RPA, and quantum computing, tomorrow's testing won't just be faster, it will be smarter, more autonomous, and deeply embedded into business processes. It has evolved from simple record-and-playback scripts into intelligent, data-driven ecosystems that drive quality across the software lifecycle. As we look ahead, several powerful forces- AI, shift-left practices, cloud-native development, and intelligent observability- are shaping the next era of automation.

This chapter explores the technologies redefining the testing landscape and provides a forward-looking perspective on how QA professionals can prepare for and embrace this evolution.

11.1 AI-Driven Testing, Low-Code Automation, and Robotic Process Automation (RPA)

11.1.1 AI-Driven Testing

Artificial intelligence is becoming integral to modern test automation. It allows systems to not only execute tests but to learn, adapt, and optimize testing workflows over time.

Key capabilities of AI in testing include:

- **Self-healing test scripts:** Automatically detect and fix broken locators or workflows (e.g., Testim, Mabl).
- **Predictive testing:** AI analyzes code changes and past failures to suggest which tests to run using machine learning (e.g., Launchable).
- **Anomaly detection:** Identify behavioral outliers in production through log analysis and telemetry.
- **Natural language test generation:** Convert business requirements or conversations into executable test scripts (e.g., Functionize, AutonomIQ).

Imagine your automation suite self-adjusting to code changes, optimizing coverage without human input. This is now possible.

11.1.2 Low-Code Test Automation

The barrier to test automation is lowering. Codeless tools now empower non-engineers, product owners, business analysts, and manual testers to contribute directly to the test suite. Low-code platforms enable teams to build and maintain test cases using drag-and-drop interfaces, reusable components, and visual workflows, without deep programming knowledge.

Benefits:

- o Empowers non-developers to contribute to test automation
- o Accelerates test script creation and modification
- o Reduces dependency on specialized automation engineers
- o Speeds up onboarding for QA teams in fast-moving environments

Popular Tools:

- o Katalon Studio, Leapwork, TestCraft, Tricentis Tosca

🔍 Low-code doesn't eliminate the need for good design, and scalable automation still requires planning and architecture.

11.1.3 Robotic Process Automation (RPA)

RPA tools, originally designed for automating business workflows, are increasingly intersecting with test automation, particularly for non-UI and legacy system interactions.

How RPA is influencing QA:

- o Automates repetitive test setup and teardown tasks
- o Simulates complex user journeys across multiple systems
- o Integrates with ERP systems, mainframes, and desktop apps
- o Enables test automation for non-web, non-API use cases

Examples:

- o Using UiPath bots to populate test data in SAP before test execution
- o Automating regression tests for desktop accounting software using "Automation Anywhere".

RPA complements traditional testing by extending automation into business-critical systems that don't expose standard APIs or web interfaces.

11.2 Quantum Computing and Its Implications for Test Automation

Quantum computing is still an emerging field, but its impact on computing, security, and algorithm complexity will eventually reshape testing strategies.

11.2.1 What is Quantum Computing?

Quantum computing leverages principles of quantum mechanics like "superposition" and "entanglement" to perform calculations far beyond the reach of classical computers.

Key advantages:

- o Solves certain problems exponentially faster
- o Ideal for optimization, cryptography, simulation, and pattern detection

- Potential to revolutionize data analysis, machine learning, and systems modeling

11.2.2 Implications for Test Automation

While quantum computing is still largely experimental, its future implications for testing could include:

- Simulating complex test environments in physics, finance, or logistics using quantum emulators
- Optimizing test coverage by analyzing millions of input combinations simultaneously
- Security testing for post-quantum encryption algorithms
- Testing quantum algorithms themselves, an entirely new QA discipline

⚠ Quantum test automation won't replace traditional testing soon, but understanding its impact now prepares QA professionals for the frontier.

11.3 Preparing for the Future of Test Automation

The future is not just about tools, it's about mindset and strategy. Testers and QA engineers can prepare by:

- Learning to work with AI tools rather than fearing them
- Developing domain knowledge, which will remain irreplaceable
- Collaborating across disciplines, Dev, QA, Ops, and business
- Investing in continuous learning, certifications, and experimentation

💬 In the future, testers won't just execute tests. They'll be data analysts, automation architects, and AI facilitators, guiding quality through complex ecosystems.

11.4 Chapter Summary

Test automation is transforming from manual script writing to autonomous intelligence; from browser clicks to AI-driven prediction; from human-only maintenance to self-healing systems. Emerging technologies like AI, low-code tools, RPA, and quantum computing are not abstract ideas. They are tools being adopted today by high-performing teams to accelerate delivery, increase coverage, and reduce risk. The best way to future-proof your career or team is to embrace these shifts early, build hybrid skills, and lead the evolution, not resist it.

REFERENCES

1. Cohn, M. (2009). *Succeeding with Agile: Software Development Using Scrum.* Addison-Wesley Professional.
2. Chelimsky, D. (2010). *et al.* The RSpec Book: Behaviour Driven Development with RSpec, Cucumber, and Friends. Pragmatic Bookshelf.
3. Meszaros, G. (2007). *xUnit Test Patterns: Refactoring Test Code.* Addison-Wesley Professional.
4. SmartBear. (2022). *BDD 101: Introduction to Behavior-Driven Development.*https://smartbear.com/learn/bdd/introduction-to-behavior-driven-development/
5. Appium Documentation. (2023). *Test Automation Frameworks and Architecture.*
6. SeleniumHQ. (2023). *The Selenium Project.* https://www.selenium.dev
7. Microsoft. (2023). *Playwright Documentation.* https://playwright.dev
8. Appium. (2023). *Appium Documentation.* https://appium.io
9. RestAssured. (2023). *Official GitHub Repository.*
10. Humble, J., & Farley, D. (2010). *Continuous Delivery: Reliable Software Releases through Build, Test, and Deployment Automation.* Addison-Wesley.
11. Jenkins. (2023). *Jenkins User Documentation.*
12. CircleCI. (2023). *CircleCI Configuration Reference.*
13. Atlassian. (2023). *What is CI/CD?*
14. Docker. (2023). *Docker for CI/CD.*
15. Ribeiro, M. (2016). *T., Singh, S., & Guestrin, C.* Why Should I Trust you? Explaining the Predictions of Any Classifier. arXiv preprint arXiv:1602.04938.
16. Testim.io. (2023). *AI-Based Test Automation.*
17. Mabl. (2023). *Intelligent Test Automation.*
18. Diffblue. (2023). *AI for Java Unit Tests.*
19. Allure TestOps. (2023). *Test Health Monitoring.*
20. GitHub Actions. (2023). *Workflow Syntax and Best Practices.*
21. GitLab Docs. (2023). *CI/CD Pipelines in GitLab.*
22. Micro Focus. (2023). *LoadRunner Overview.*
23. ThoughtWorks. (2022). *Performance Testing in DevOps.*
24. Functionize. (2023). *What is Self-Healing Automation?*
25. Ribeiro, M. (2016). *T., Singh, S., & Guestrin, C.* Why Should I Trust you? Explaining the Predictions of Any Classifier. arXiv preprint arXiv:1602.04938.
26. Google Testing Blog. (2022). *Flaky Tests and How to Fix Them.*
27. Berihun, N. (2023). *G., Dongmo, C., & Van der Poll, J. A.* The applicability of automated testing frameworks for mobile application testing: A systematic literature review. Computers, 12(5), 97.
28. Garousi, V., Keleş, A. (2021). *B., Balaman, Y., Güler, Z. Ö., & Arcuri, A.* Model-based testing in practice: An experience report from the web applications domain. arXiv preprint arXiv:2104.02152.

29. Ferreira, M., Viegas, L., Faria, J. (2025). *P., & Lima, B.* Acceptance test generation with large language models: An industrial case study. arXiv preprint arXiv:2504.07244.

30. IBM Research. (2023). *Quantum Computing Overview.*

31. Functionize. (2023). *What is Self-Healing Automation?*

32. Leapwork. (2023). *Low-Code Test Automation Platform.*

33. UiPath. (2023). *RPA in Software Testing.*

34. Bitbucket. (2023). *Bitbucket Pipelines Overview.*

35. Launchable. (2023). *Test Impact Analysis Using Machine Learning.*

36. Cypress Docs. (2023). *Handling Flaky Tests.*

37. ThoughtWorks. (2023). *Refactoring Automation in Agile.*

38. Applitools. (2023). *Selenium vs.* Cypress vs Playwright: Choosing the Right Web Testing Tool.

✍ LEAVE A REVIEW

Thank you for reading!

I truly appreciate you taking the time to read Mastering Test Automation: A Practical Guide to Scalable and Efficient Testing.

If you found this book helpful, I would be incredibly grateful if you could take a moment to leave an honest review on Amazon.

Your feedback not only helps other readers discover this book, but it also supports independent authors like me in continuing to share practical, real-world knowledge.

You can leave your review here: https://amzn.eu/d/ezgKfDn

Thank you again for your time and support!

👤 ABOUT THE AUTHOR

Chizitere Sylvia Olebu is a data-driven problem solver with a background in finance, data science, and software quality assurance.

She has worked across industries in roles spanning customer insights, business intelligence, and QA, combining analytical depth with hands-on testing experience. Her transition into tech was fueled by a passion for automation, efficiency, and getting things right the first time.

In Mastering Test Automation, Sylvia shares practical strategies and tools that reflect her real-world work across both corporate and technical landscapes. She's committed to helping others bridge the gap between theory and practice, especially those new to test automation.

When she's not analyzing data or improving test pipelines, she enjoys writing, continuous learning, and mentoring others on their journey into tech.

www.ingramcontent.com/pod-product-compliance
Lightning Source LLC
LaVergne TN
LVHW052322060326
832902LV00023B/4558